# We Need to Talk!

## *Stop Interfering*

© **Copyright 2015 by Darryl Bumpass Sr - All rights reserved.**

This document is geared towards providing exact and reliable information in regards to the topic and issue covered. The publication is sold with the idea that the publisher is not required to render accounting, officially permitted, or otherwise, qualified services. If advice is necessary, legal or professional, a practiced individual in the profession should be ordered.

- From a Declaration of Principles which was accepted and approved equally by a Committee of the American Bar Association and a Committee of Publishers and Associations.

In no way is it legal to reproduce, duplicate, or transmit any part of this document by either electronic means or in printed format. Recording of this publication is strictly prohibited and any storage of this document is not allowed unless with written permission from the publisher. All rights reserved.

The information provided herein is stated to be truthful and consistent, in that any liability, in terms of inattention or otherwise, by any usage or abuse of any policies, processes, or directions contained within is the solitary and utter responsibility of the recipient reader. Under no circumstances will any legal responsibility or blame be held against the publisher for any reparation, damages, or monetary loss due to the information herein, either directly or indirectly.

Respective authors own all copyrights not held by the publisher.

The information herein is offered for informational purposes solely, and is universal as so. The presentation of the information is without contract or any type of guarantee assurance.

The trademarks that are used are without any consent, and the publication of the trademark is without permission or backing by the trademark owner. All trademarks and brands within this book are for clarifying purposes only and are owned by the owners themselves, not affiliated with this document.

# Contents

Introduction ..................................................................................................1

## Chapter 1: We Need to Talk! .................................................................2
Never apologize for being who you are ...............................................2
Apologize for not being who you are ..................................................3
Learn to value yourself ........................................................................4
You are here to reach the stars ............................................................5

## Chapter 2: Stop Interfering ...................................................................6
Developing, not interfering ..................................................................6
4 signs that you are depriving yourself from success and happiness ....7
How to stop interfering ........................................................................8

## Chapter 3: As If! ....................................................................................10
As if ....................................................................................................10
As if – exercise ...................................................................................11
Don't be your own enemy ..................................................................12
Be a leader .........................................................................................13
Stepping out of your cage ..................................................................14
Refusing to settle for less ..................................................................14
Know the rules before you play the game ........................................15

## Chapter 4: Process & Progress ............................................................17
Making steady progress .....................................................................17

## Chapter 5: Homework ..........................................................................19
Becoming responsible .......................................................................19
So let it be written, so let it be done .................................................20

## Chapter 6: New Chapter, New Level ..................................................22
How to work smarter .........................................................................22
Making a life-changing decision .......................................................23
7 ways to make life-changing decisions ...........................................23

Conclusion ................................................................................................25

About the Author .....................................................................................26

# Introduction

Thank you for downloading my book, *"We Need to Talk! Stop Interfering."*

This book will take you along the road to discovery. The Universe is constantly shifting and changing, and we shift with it. What matters is on what side of the shift we want to be. The correct side is the discovery side and this book explains how to take that road of discovery in order to become the best you can be.

*We Need to Talk!* shows you how to accomplish great things in your life and offers guidance through self-acceptance. In order to improve yourself and your life, you have to accept who you already are.

This book teaches you about the power of self-acceptance, responsibility and decision-making.

Every person is destined to do great things and with true guidance, motivation, and effort, you can accomplish a lot.

If you have ever wanted to change something in your life and become even better, there is no reason to wait. Start now.

*Get Your Shift Together!*

# Chapter 1: We Need to Talk!

The universe is shifting. You have to decide on what side of the shift you are going to be, the recovery side or the discovery side. The discovery side includes discovering the new you, discovering why you are here and discovering your destiny. My book *"I Know You Hear Me, But Are You Listening?"* explores the beginning of your recovery and how to start asking the right questions. This book is the beginning of your discovery. Get Your Shift Together!

Regardless of whether we like it or not, the entire world is constantly changing. It is in our nature to change with it. However, people usually consider change as something bad. The most frequent reason for refusing to change is, *"I don't want to lose my personality"* or *"I like being myself"*. The biggest problem about these statements is their perspectives. The path to discovery requires certain changes to be made. These changes aren't a negative thing. Changes aren't about losing yourself or becoming a new person. Change is the way of upgrading yourself in order to become the best you can be. That is a marvelous thing. It is in our nature to constantly progress and improve.

## *Never apologize for being who you are*

As it was mentioned above, in order to shift with the universe and discover how to become the best you can be, you have to progress. This progress isn't about becoming a new person, it is about improving yourself.

In order to achieve these things, you must be happy with who you are now. That is important because if you are not happy with yourself now, you won't appreciate everything you can become – and there is no reason not be happy with yourself. You are a smart, driven person who possesses a lot of potential to achieve great things in your life.

There will always be people who undermine someone's success. You should, immediately, know it's not about you. When someone undermines your achievements, it is the reflection of their own insecurities. You should always strive to be yourself and only then you will progress and become everything you have dreamed of.

*"To help yourself, you must be yourself. Be the best you can be. When you make a mistake, learn from it, pick yourself up, and move on."*

Dave Pelzer

Self-respect is crucial for all aspects of your life. Regardless of what you do, where you are, and who you are with, you have to respect yourself. The truth is people who don't respect themselves cannot respect other people as well. That goes hand in hand.

## *Apologize for not being who you are*

Having role models is perfectly okay. Some scientists even say it is healthy to have a person to whom you can look up. We want to accomplish great things just like they have, and we often identify ourselves with them, for example, if that person also had a difficult childhood or if they overcame a big obstacle. The problem arises when the person mimics another person. Trying to become someone else doesn't result in happiness. True happiness occurs when we develop our personality and progress gradually.

Therefore, before you start on your road to discovery, you should first apologize to yourself for not being who you are. The most common reason for ignoring our wishes, preferences, and abilities is low self-esteem and a negative mindset which makes us believe we are not capable of achieving something. That's wrong. Every person on this planet is born to do great things. The only difference is in the approach.

You can get rid of a negative mindset with mantras. They are phrases which serve as positive affirmations. You should find your own mantra and repeat it to yourself whenever you can. Also, when you are saying your mantra, you really have to believe in every word. Soon enough, you will change your opinion of yourself. Here are some mantras for you:

- *I have no reason to want to be someone I'm not.*
- *I am smart and capable of anything.*
- *I will and want to become even better.*
- *I am born to do great things.*

## *Learn to value yourself*

Now that we've established that you should never be someone you're not, but always strive to be who you are in order to become happy and the best you can be, you have to learn how to value yourself. Here are some tips for learning how to appreciate yourself:

- ***Don't compare yourself with others*** – as I already mentioned, you are perfectly capable to do great things in life, and the only way to do that is by appreciating yourself. Comparing yourself with others won't make you happy and it will not help you progress. People usually measure their self-worth by comparing themselves with other people, instead of analyzing their own potential. *"Peace comes from within. Do not seek it without."* Buddha

- ***Don't worry about whether others will accept you*** – let's face it, you can't make everyone happy. As soon as you acknowledge that, it will be easier for you to focus on yourself. You can try and try, and there will still be people who won't like something. That is okay. You are not here to please every person around you. You are here to succeed in all aspects of your life.

- ***Recognize that you are a valuable person*** – you are a valuable person just by the fact you exist. What you need to do is to recognize it, believe in it, and build on it. If you don't think you're a valuable person because you made some mistakes, then you should quit right now. You are human, just like me, and you make mistakes, just like me. Mistakes don't define us. *"To err is human..."* Alexander Pope

- ***Do the best with what you have*** – one common characteristic of all successful people, regardless of their niche or background, is the fact they always do the best with what they have, regardless of the circumstances. We value ourselves more when we do our best in every situation. If you don't do your best, later you feel guilty because you know you could have done more. Fulfilling all your potential makes you a better and smarter person. It's like playing a game; you can't start with a new level if you didn't get all points in the current one.

- **You are unique and that's a great thing** – there are no two completely same people on this planet; even twins only have appearance in common. When it comes to character, we are all different. That uniqueness should be embraced. Every person – you, me, someone else – has unique abilities that we have to discover in order to accomplish something. Embrace yourself.

## You are here to reach the stars

*"Per aspera ad astra."*

*Through hardships to the stars,* the meaning of the Latin proverb written above, applies perfectly to struggles that all of us have to reach the stars. The reason why you are reading my book now is because you want to reach the stars; you want to become successful. After all, we are all here for a reason.

Hard work pays off, and all hardships lead to the stars, you just have to be determined to try it. Since you are reading my words now, you already started your discovery.

You are here because you have a purpose in this world. Our existence should be meaningful; we aren't here just to breathe air only, and we are here to use all our potential. Developing as a person is what we all are here for; it benefits us and the people around us. You are destined to reach the stars and be the best version of yourself and the primary aim of this book is to show you how to do that.

*"All our dreams can come true if we have the courage to pursue them."*
Walt Disney

# Chapter 2: Stop Interfering

Here is the truth: our blueprint has been drawn out for us before we were even born. And we should stop interfering with it. Every person is here due to one special purpose – that is to discover yourself and continuously improve yourself throughout your life. Every person has a different blueprint, but what we all have in common is the fact that we can do spectacular things. These things can be done only after you are aware of your own potential. In other words, in order to discover what you bring or how much you can accomplish, you have to embrace what you are now. You shouldn't interfere with your own potential and ambitions; you should strive to develop them.

*"You were put on this earth to achieve your greatest self, to live out your purpose, and to do it courageously."*

Steve Maraboli

## *Developing, not interfering*

There is more to you than the image you see in your mirror. Even the image you see in your mirror can be misleading sometimes. For example, you convince yourself that you are either too thin or a little bit overweight, that you want different arms, legs, even hair. However, in order to develop, you should stop interfering with yourself. You should embrace every single aspect of your personality and physical appearance.

You can only achieve everything from your blueprint by being free. Freedom comes from within. Freedom doesn't accept a negative attitude, limitations, self-criticism, and low self-esteem. Freedom is the result of positive vibes, self-support, confidence, and determination to do great things in life.

Controlling the situation is the only way to rise from it and make it better. On the other hand, when we interfere with certain situations numerous problems can arise. These are the facts of life, and they can be applied to us. If you are preventing yourself from moving forward then you will never be happy. The only way to move forward is to allow yourself to rise and be the best you can be.

Let the artists motivate you; the only way they were able to create their masterpieces was because they didn't interfere with their own talent and thoughts. They just expressed them and that is what you should do – you should express your thoughts, talents, and other abilities in your own way, not hide them.

*"The best road to progress is freedom's road."*

John F. Kennedy

## *4 signs that you are depriving yourself from achieving success and happiness*

The problem is, we often interfere with our blueprint without even being aware of it. That happens when we go through several bad experiences in our lives that shape our mindset. Here are some signs that you are interfering with your own success and happiness:

- **You are suppressing positive emotions** – this is the most common sign of depriving yourself from happiness and success. Whenever you feel something positive, e.g., optimism about the positive outcome of some project, or just being happy, you try to suppress it. There is a reason for it. You suppress positive emotions because you don't want to be disappointed in case you fail. But let me tell you something – we all fail sometimes. That is perfectly okay. Failures are a part of life and you should treat them as lessons. The key is to turn every negative into positive. Your life can significantly change by expressing positive emotions, instead of suppressing them. Allow yourself to be happy, because you deserve it.

- **Happiness anxiety** – that was the term coined by late Nathaniel Branden, a psychotherapist known for his work in the psychology of self-esteem. Happiness anxiety happens when you feel nervous when you are happy because you believe happiness doesn't last and something will ruin it. That's life; good things happen and bad things happen, too. Instead of feeling nervous and anticipating something that may come along and ruin your happiness, you should reassure yourself that regardless of what comes along you will be prepared to deal with it. You earned your happiness, and it would be wrong not to feel it.

- ***You are too distracted*** – this happens when you have to deal with a lot of commitments and tasks. People make a lot of commitments because they want to achieve more. Unfortunately, that's not what happens. Too many commitments lead to distraction, and distraction decreases your productivity. In order to be productive and succeed in everything you want to do, you have to take one step at a time. When you finish one project, assignment, or commitment, take on the next one and so on.

- ***Self-criticism*** – is your biggest enemy. People sometimes don't even realize that they are their own arch nemesis. Instead of criticizing everything you do, you should acknowledge all the good things about yourself and what you do. Learn to love and appreciate yourself. Self-criticism interferes with your personal growth. In order to stop interfering with it, you should love yourself. Only when you love and appreciate yourself will you be able to love and appreciate others. There is no difference between you and me. I am able to do great things in my life because I know my values and I know what I am capable of, and you should do the same. It's not difficult; try it.

## How to stop interfering

Here are some tips on how to stop interfering with your own blueprint:

- Begin your day with love – start every day by reminding yourself how much you are worth.
- Take some time every day to focus on your thoughts, preferences and desires.
- Never suppress your feelings.
- Expand your interests – improving yourself and your knowledge is always a great way to progress.
- Make memories – do something you have always wanted to do.
- Surrender yourself to all your ideas.
- Let your personality and spirituality grow.

- Own your own potential – the key to stop interfering is to love yourself and acknowledge that you possess limitless potential to accomplish everything you want. Don't hide if you want to achieve it.
- Be patient – never rush yourself to do anything. Urgency and fear aren't your friends. Trust in yourself, work hard and be motivated and you will get everything done.
- Appreciate your thoughts, talents, desires, and everything around you.
- Trust your intuition; don't ignore it.
- Never participate in activities that bring you down. Only strive to do what is beneficial to your honor and respect.
- Accept the uncertainty – you never know what can happen, and I think that's a good thing. Not knowing is part of the fun; it gives you the freedom to enjoy the present day and do everything you can to have a pleasant tomorrow.
- Forgive yourself – if you constantly blame yourself for everything, you will prevent yourself from moving forward. Always forgive yourself for your mistakes. They are just lessons, remember.
- Be real – always be honest to yourself and other people.
- Focus on the positive, not the negative.

# Chapter 3: As If!

*What do you want to do in your life? What do you want to accomplish? What person do you want to become?*

These are the questions that are of huge importance for your life but you rarely ask yourself or try to find an answer. Instead, you just say stuff like *If only I could, I would even settle for_____*, and *I wish I could just do\_\_\_\_*.

That just means you sell yourself short and you have to stop doing that. You should aim for the maximum, not for mediocrity. People are satisfied with mediocrity because aiming high seems risky. When you dream big, the first step tends to be invisible, because you don't know where to begin. When you know what your first step should be, it is easier to accomplish what you want.

## *As if*

Yes, *As if* is your first step. You have to start acting as if you are already living and loving the life you always dream about.

> "Faith is taking the first step even when you don't see the whole staircase."
> 
> Martin Luther King Jr.

The first step out of the mediocrity zone into fulfilling your maximum potential is being the person you wanted to become, doing what you see yourself doing, and living the life you always dream about. Is there any reason for you to wait? No. Change is possible and it has to start now.

Regardless of what person you want to be, you have to start acting like that person now. For example, if you want to become a successful businessman, you have to act like you are one right now. *Why?* It's because when you act like you are a successful businessman, you will think like one, and then, you will be motivated and work hard to achieve everything you wanted. Regardless of what you already do, you have to act like you are what you always wanted to become. If you work in a grocery store and always pictured yourself as a business manager, who says you can't do that? You can start now. Get involved in every aspect of the job, work hard, be motivated and it will happen. Hard work pays off, and every single one of us can succeed in life with a bit of determination, the right strategy, and motivation.

## As if – exercise

- ***Visualize it*** – now or later when you have 20 minutes or even more, really think about what you want to do, who you want to become and what you want to accomplish. You should clearly visualize it and be truthful to yourself. Regardless of what is it, there is no reason to feel embarrassed, silly, or shy about it. It is your own preference and your own mind. For example, *I want to become a best-selling author, I want to work for a high profile tech company, I want to_____*

- ***Feel the visualization*** – now, when you've visualized what you want to do, accomplish and become, try to live that in your mind. You should visualize as many details as possible in order to truly feel everything you see. For example, *how do you talk, carry yourself, walk every day, what do you do every day, how do you start your day, what's your schedule like and how do you organize your day* and try to answer these questions like the person you see when you visualize it.

- ***Do it, be it*** – live your life exactly how you saw it in the previous two steps. You should act like the person from your visualizations, because that person is the real you. You saw that and you visualized it because you kept digging deep down and the image you saw is a reflection of the real you. Remember, *as if*.

- ***Own it*** – I believe that it's impossible to be, do, or accomplish something you don't believe in. Therefore, if you want to accomplish something, you have to firmly believe in it. For example, if you want to become a best-selling author, you have to live and act like you are. But most of all, you have to believe that you have the potential to be it. That will help you with your writing; you will be motivated and you will have a mindset of the successful author.

- ***Repeat***.

Acting *as if* really isn't difficult and from my experience, this brings a significant change to your life. Don't miss it.

## Don't be your own enemy

We usually get caught up on what someone else is doing to us instead of concentrating on what we are doing to ourselves. As I already mentioned, you cannot compare yourself with others, and you shouldn't strive to please everyone (because that's just not going to happen). There will always be someone who will say something negative or do something negative, but they just show their own insecurities with these actions. Instead, you should think about what you are doing to yourself. Sometimes we can harm ourselves without even realizing it. For example, every time you think about what someone else did, you are harming yourself. That happens because you are blaming yourself for that situation. Stop that and be happy. Here are some things you should stop doing to yourself:

- ***Stop running from your problems*** – when you avoid your problems you are just prolonging them. Sooner or later you will have to face them, and it's better to do that sooner. After all, when you solve one problem you will know how to avoid it from occurring in the future, which is another valuable lesson.

- ***Stop procrastinating*** - you are an adult and you have to make sure you finish all your projects, assignments or other commitments in a timely manner.

- ***Stop lying to yourself*** – you should be able to trust and rely on yourself. There is no point in lying to yourself because that affects your entire life. Don't tell yourself you can't do something just because you are afraid of failure. If you can do it, then go ahead.

- ***Stop living in the past*** – this is the most common mistake that people make. They live in the past and refuse to let go. Moving on doesn't mean forgetting what happened or what you went through, it means using your past experiences to make a better future.

- ***Don't buy happiness; earn it*** – don't try to buy happiness through shoes, gadgets, clothes, etc. because it's not going to happen. These things can make you happy for a little while, but your happiness should be earned. Happiness is when you know you accomplished something with your own work. Happiness is when you know you are the best you can be and that you're living the life you always wanted.

- ***Don't rely on others*** – you should only rely on yourself because you can't expect other people to do important things for you and you are perfectly capable of doing them yourself. After all, you are intelligent, have potential that has to be used, and nothing is stopping you from doing something yourself. As I already mentioned, never pay too much attention to what other people do or say to you. There will always be someone who wants to bring you down, but your job is to not let them do that.

- ***Stop hating yourself*** – we can be tough on ourselves. When something goes wrong, we blame ourselves. When someone says something bad to us, we think it's true. When you stop doing that, things can significantly change. There is no reason to hate yourself or to think someone else is better. *Why would someone be better than you?* You have your own potential that you should use, and you can accomplish everything you want.

## Be a leader

*"The function of leadership is to produce more leaders, not more followers."*

Ralph Nader

You have to move from your position of a follower into a position of a leader. You have to lead your life, not be led. The first step towards becoming a leader is to admit there is something that needs improvement. And the truth is, we all need to constantly improve. There is nothing wrong with that. Human beings have survived so far only because they constantly improved and adapted to every situation. I know you might feel broken inside and feel like you aren't good enough, but that's false. Every person is valuable and that's not just a phrase used by various websites to promote their services. It is the truth. What you need in your life is the courage to accept the fact that you progress with improvements. This will help you take control of your own life instead of letting others do that for you. It is your life and you should live it and achieve everything you want. After all, people who are afraid of dying haven't really lived. It is always better to be brave and do things that make us happy. Only when we are happy will we be able to make other people happy as well.

## Stepping out of your cage

In order to act *as if* and become a leader in your life, not a follower, you need to step out of your comfort zone. Here are some tips on how you can do that:

- ***Do everyday things differently*** – this is a great start for people who find it difficult to step out of their cage. For example, start by taking a different route to work, going to a different supermarket to buy groceries, or become a vegetarian for one day. Sometimes, some seemingly unimportant things can help us achieve big ones.

- ***Take your time to make decisions*** – take your time to observe what is going on; think about all the benefits you would gain in doing something differently.

- ***Trust yourself when making snap decisions*** – as I mentioned, you should trust yourself in every situation.

- ***Small steps*** – if you are a person who finds it difficult to step out of your comfort zone, then try baby steps. Don't try to do everything differently at once – go step by step and you will get there.

## Refusing to settle for less

Acting as if you are living the life you always dreamed of means you shouldn't settle for mediocrity. Complacency should never be your norm. Wanting only the best from your job, relationship, and life in general isn't unrealistic. It is *normal*. It is perfectly normal to want the best thing for yourself and your family. When you know what you want, you will find a way to get it. It's very simple.

There is no reason to settle for mediocrity when excellence is within you. Here is why you should only strive to get the best out of your life and relationships:

- Mediocrity doesn't lead to happiness.
- We pass mediocrity on to our children.
- Mediocrity doesn't pay off.
- It means we don't respect ourselves.
- It means a lack of motivation and desire.
- Life is too short to settle for anything less than what we truly deserve.
- Settling for less means you are lying to yourself.

Avoid settling for less with these tips:

- Step out of your comfort zone.
- Realize your full potential and do something about it.
- Acknowledge you are completely capable of accomplishing what you desire.
- Never focus on negative people.
- Less excuses, more action.
- Every day do something that will make your life a little bit better.
- Never feel guilty for doing anything that makes your life better.
- Respect people around you.
- Leave people who don't respect you.
- Choose mantras for this occasion as well. Say every day: *You haven't seen anything yet. You deserve the best and you can get it.*

## *Know the rules before you play the game*

Throughout this chapter, I wrote about acting *as if* in order to be the best you can be. You have seen how to do that and learned *as if* includes stepping out of your comfort zone and not settling for less. Here are some rules you need to know to become the leader and master *as if* to make your own life the best it can be:

- **Take 100% responsibility** –regardless of what you do or what you want to accomplish in your life, you should always take responsibility for your actions.

- **Know why you are here** – this is why *Chapter 2* is important. You should stop interfering with your blueprint and potential in order to embrace the role of a leader. You have your goals and you know your purpose is to constantly improve yourself; be very clear about that and constantly work towards that goal.

- ***Be detailed about what you want*** – the most common reason why people fail to get what they want is because they aren't detailed about it. This is why you needed to know the power of visualization and acting *as if*. This practice helps you discover and determine all the details about your goals that you can accomplish. The more details you know, the easier it is.

- ***NOTHING is impossible***.

- ***Have faith in yourself***.

- ***Make goal-setting your habit***.

*"Leaders are made, they are not born. They are made by hard effort, which is the price which all of us must pay to achieve any goal that is worthwhile."*

Vince Lombardi

# Chapter 4: Process & Progress

*"If you are walking down the right path and you're willing to keep walking, eventually you'll make progress."*

Barack Obama

There are no great achievements without continuous progress. It is impossible to do nothing and expect a change. In order to have a better life or become more successful, we still have to go through certain processes and progress. That is our own evolution but in the end it will pay off. If you are adamant to find the right person for you and get married, then you will do everything to find that person. When you want business success, then you will find a way to accomplish that. That *way* is the process and progress that is inevitable.

Remember, nothing happens overnight and we have to work for the best things in our lives.

## *Making steady progress*

Process and progress towards achieving great things in all aspects of your life doesn't have to be too difficult. Here are some tips for making steady progress:

- **Commit to the long haul** – regardless of the goal, your success depends on how much effort you put in it. Therefore, you should be in it for long haul and refuse to give up.

- **Working on accomplishing your goal should be routine** – when you decide to make a change in your life and improve your lifestyle and enrich your personality, you have to constantly work on achieving that goal. It should be part of your everyday life. Don't find yourself a few months from now realizing you lost sight of what you wanted to accomplish.

- ***See the big picture*** – whenever you feel like you aren't doing so well, stop for a while and think how far you've come. When you realize what you accomplished and how much your life has changed, that will motivate you to carry on. After all, when you want to improve something, every step, even the smallest one during that process has a significant impact in your life.

- ***Evaluate your progress*** – from time to time evaluate everything you've done during your progress to achieve a certain goal. This will help you come up with an accurate plan about what you should do next. If needed, make tiny adjustments, because progress isn't a straight line, and your job is to make sure that whenever some adjustments are needed, you are willing to correct that line and move on.

- ***Consider obstacles as challenges*** – I wouldn't be able to succeed and write my second book if I gave in when faced with each obstacle. You shouldn't, either. Obstacles are just challenges. If you go past them successfully, great. If not, you had a valuable lesson to learn. Always try to see something positive in every situation.

- ***Celebrate the progress*** – any type of progress is reason to celebrate. And yes, you can celebrate it before you reach your goal. The sole fact that you decided to accomplish something bigger is a big move and you should appreciate yourself for that.

- ***Get a life coach*** – if you really feel like you need more guidance, but have a clear vision, then you should consult a life coach and he or she will provide their assistance. Every life coach should have a website where you can see whether they are the right coach for you. My website, www.darrylbumpasssr.com contains a wide range of examples where people who need guidance can immediately see whether I am the right coach for them. If you don't see that on the coach's website, contact them and ask them about what you are interested in. However, make sure the person you work with has credentials and positive reviews from other people.

- ***Associate the pleasure with progress*** – when you are in the process of achieving some goal you can get even more motivation by associating the current progress with great pleasure. For example, imagine how the accomplishment would make you feel. It would make you happy, excited and confident, right? Then work towards making yourself feel that way.

# Chapter 5: Homework

Everyone can accomplish everything they dream of. Right now, you are next in line for your very own miracle and your next step should be moving in front of that line. That's not as difficult as you think it is.

In order to move in front of that line and finally make your miracle come true you have to be responsible. I mentioned responsibility a few times already, and for a good reason. Where there is no responsibility, there is no miracle or accomplishment. All your hard work won't pay off if you aren't responsible.

Therefore, your homework is:

- To become responsible.
- To write down all your goals.

## *Becoming responsible*

*"The greatest day in your life and mine is when we take total responsibility for our attitudes. That's the day we truly grow up."*

John C. Maxwell

Becoming responsible has plenty of benefits. For example: everyone respects you; your reputation improves; your loved ones appreciate you more; if you're single it will be easier for you to find a loved one; you will be first in line for promotion at work, etc. So, here are some tips on how to become more responsible:

- **Awareness** – be aware of the fact that everything you do is your responsibility, regardless of the result. Everything you're doing is enriching your experience and hence requires 100% responsibility for every possible outcome.

- ***Control*** – acknowledging the fact that you are in charge for your overall experience (regardless of what experience) lets you take control of it and make sure you minimize the risks.

- ***Act; don't react*** – don't be a person who just reacts to something that happens around them. Be the person who is willing to change things. Be active, not passive. After all, only by acting (as if) you can take control of your life and situations in it. It is foolish to make mistakes over and over again but expect the same results.

- ***Admit past mistakes and move on*** – admit the fact that most negative experiences in your life happened because you didn't believe in yourself more. For example, you were so determined you won't get that job and you didn't do your best to impress the employer. Admitting your negative thinking got in your way means that you are taking responsibility and you are willing to change that.

- ***Don't let the fear control you*** – take a deep breath, and think about that fear. Is it rational or irrational? More than 90% of the fears we have are irrational. They are just products of our mind; don't let them prevent you from accomplishing great things.

## So let it be written, so let it be done

The importance of writing things down is undeniable. When we write important things down, we are more focused and we know where we're going.

Harvard University conducted a study in 1979 to determine how writing things down affects our lives. The results of the study showed that people who wrote down their goals for the future (3% of them) earned ten times as much money as the rest of their class. This is why you need to write down all your goals. Even if you think they are meaningless, write them down. Additionally, make sure you check up on what you wrote from time to time and you will see how much you accomplished and what to do next, and you'll know how to get it.

Writing things down works because you create a clear vision of your success. When that vision is clear, you can feel it and you'll work hard to achieve it. Here are some tips for writing down your goals:

- ***Create a clear vision*** – think about what you really want. If you don't know what you want then you won't know how to get there. Start by answering these questions: *What does my ideal life look like? Where I can see myself living in 5 years? What do I really want to create for myself?* Try to be specific and write everything down in a manner that is easy to read and understand.

- ***Choose an achievable timeframe for your goals*** – when you know what your goal is, it is easy to know how much time you will need to accomplish it. Write that down as well.

- ***Set milestones*** – divide your goal into several different milestones. These milestones will be easier to accomplish and when you successfully complete your current milestone, you will be more motivated to start with a new one.

# Chapter 6: New Chapter, New Level

It's our human nature to strive to be faster, better and wiser than the next guy. How do we accomplish that? We accomplish that with information that allows us to work smarter, not harder.

Your new chapter means starting to work smarter in order to accomplish great things.

## *How to work smarter*

- Make a *don't do* list – it contains all things you shouldn't and won't waste your time on.
- Carry notebook and pen and write down all the ideas you think of during the day. You can do it in your phone or tablet as well.
- Be able to explain who you are and what you do in 30 seconds or less. Practice that every day.
- Establish a daily ritual that will help ease your mind.
- Establish a ritual by ending every work day in the same way, to reduce stress.
- Get used to uncertainty, ambiguity and volatility. Bad things can happen. That's the circle of life. Life consists of good things and bad things, good moments and bad moments.
- Learn – ask questions, try to improve yourself, learn from people with more experience, and go to conferences. One learns throughout their life. Learning makes you smarter, and when you are smarter, you accomplish more.
- Failing is okay; not failing is impossible.
- Treat your calendar with respect; don't schedule things you don't want to do and make sure you do all the things that you said you would.
- Don't be paranoid.
- Respond to all calls, messages, and emails in a timely manner. People don't like to wait, and neither do you.
- Choose one day of the week when you don't work.
- Take breaks – you can't do everything at once. Several breaks of 10 minutes will improve your productivity.

## *Making a life-changing decision*

You can't start a new chapter without making a life-changing decision. That means you are truly ready to move on. There is nothing to be nervous about or to be scared about. Life-changing decisions are a good thing and they are the reason you will accomplish your goals.

When you make this decision, regardless of what it is, you have to try hard to achieve it. It's one thing to make a promise and another to actually do it.

*"Performance speaks louder than words."*

Tony Robbins

Most life-changing decisions are about financial situations. Everyone wants financial stability, and there's nothing wrong with that. Improving your financial situation is beneficial for all aspects of your life. If you want to find a better-paying job, nothing is stopping you. You can do it while still working at your current job.

I am sure you are tired of constantly saying *"If only I knew then what I know now"* when you think about past goals you had and how many times you missed an opportunity to change something. Well, I'm telling you, it's never too late to start a new chapter of your book. This new chapter comes with blank pages, and it depends on you how these pages will be written.

### *7 ways to make life-changing decisions*

1. Realize the power of decision making – acknowledge all the benefits of that decision. Focus only on the positives.

2. Trust your gut instinct – people usually ignore their gut instinct because they think it's wrong. Trust your gut and go with it. If something inside you is telling you to accept that promotion or to go to a job interview, start writing your own book – go with it.

3. Act on your decision – when you make your life-changing decision, make sure you carry it out until the very end. Trust me; you will appreciate yourself more. Sometimes people don't even realize how much potential they really have.

4. Inform others about your decision – it's a life-changing decision, after all. Plus, your loved ones and friends will help you achieve your goal even faster.

5. Learn from your past decisions – the chances are high that you made a lot of these decisions in the past but gave up. Use these experiences to learn from them and accomplish this one. For example, *what made you give up your last decision?* Think about what it is, and you will know what to do next.

6. Be flexible – one goal can be realized in many different ways. If you see your current approach isn't working, try the next one. There are many ways to accomplish something, not just one.

7. Have fun – enjoy the entire process. You should embrace every opportunity, every step of the way.

*"A real decision is measured by the fact that you've taken a new action. If there's no action, you haven't truly decided."*

Tony Robbins

# Conclusion

I want to thank you again for downloading my book. I hope the book motivated you to take the final step towards great accomplishments in your life.

All you have to do in order to accomplish everything you've dreamed of is to believe in yourself. When you believe in your own potential and abilities, you are able to do great things.

The purpose of this book was to inform you about the power of change and how to acknowledge your own personality and abilities. You are a valuable and remarkable person and there is no reason not to show that to the whole world.

Start your discovery now and work towards the accomplishment of your goals. I know you can do it.

If you liked the content of this book, please feel free to rate and review it.

Also, make sure you visit my official website where you can also purchase my first book, *I Know You Hear Me, But Are You Listening?*

http://darrylbumpasssr.com/

*Thank you.*

# About the Author

*Born in the Bronx area of New York City, Darryl Bumpass Sr is a dynamic motivational speaker with over 30 years of experience in entrepreneurship and leadership as well as being a Certified Professional Life Coach and mentor. A #1 Amazon Best-Selling Author, his book, "I Know You Hear Me, But Are You Listening?" examined the exercises and habits that would transform others' lives in every way possible. A satisfied reader praised the book,*

> "The motivational public speaker and certified life coach writes in a most approachable manner about what it takes to enjoy the process of self-mastery. Inspirational by all means the self-help book is a quick read poised to change the reader forever. Dedicated to bolstering how people view the pursuit of their dreams Bumpass is a veritable author, teacher and new-found friend to all who spends a few moments with his resourceful words."

*As a seasoned professional, Darryl is focused on the continuous improvement of performance, processes, people, and technology to accomplish strategic initiatives and achieve organizational goals. Darryl is a talented and popular public, inspirational, transformational and keynote speaker as well as a branding and marketing expert. As the CEO of Moneta Menswear, he adds successful fashion designer to his list of achievements. Darryl's experience in diverse industries and functions repeatedly yields exceptional results, with his lectures consistently rated as 'Exceeded Expectations' by his audiences.*

*Darryl currently lives in New York City with his wife of 26 years and their two children. When he is not writing or motivating others to the best they can be, he enjoys golf, flying helicopters, reading and traveling.*

www.ingramcontent.com/pod-product-compliance
Lightning Source LLC
Chambersburg PA
CBHW080925170426
43201CB00016B/2269